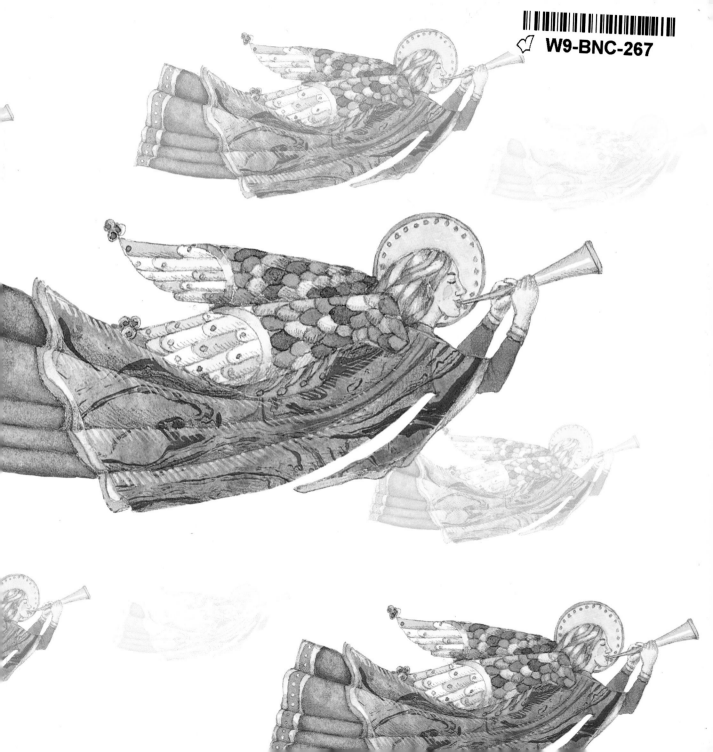

First published in North America in 1998 by
Loyola Press
3441 North Ashland Avenue
Chicago, Illinois 60657

Acknowledgments
Prayers on pages 5, 8, 13, 14, 16, 21, 22 and 24 by Joyce Denham

Carmina Gadelica
Scottish Academic Press, collected and translated by Alexander Carmichael
(page 10 from Volume I, page 105; page 12 from Volume III, page 195; page 18 from Volume III,
 page 267; page 20 from Volume III, page 77; page 23 from Volume III, page 333);

Early Irish Lyrics: eighth to twelfth century
Edited with translation, notes and glossary by Gerard Murphy, Oxford,
at the Clarendon Press, 1956, reproduced by permission of Oxford University Press;

The Poem-Book of the Gael: Translations from Irish Gaelic poetry into English prose and verse
Selected and edited by Eleanor Hull
London: Chatto & Windus, 1913.

Printed and bound in Singapore

ISBN 0-8294-1077-5

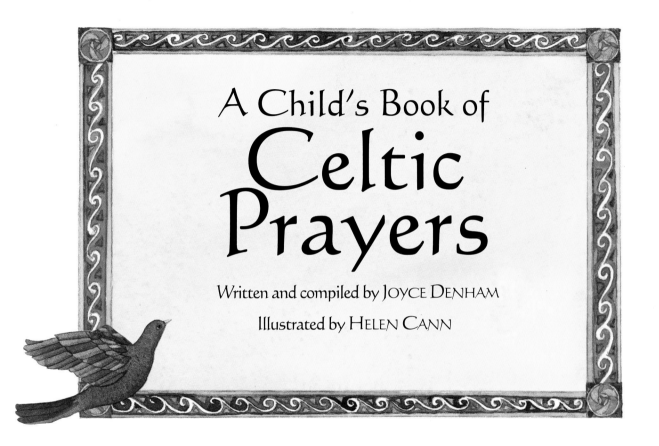

A Child's Book of
Celtic
Prayers

Written and compiled by JOYCE DENHAM

Illustrated by HELEN CANN

 Loyola Press

A Celtic Childhood

The boy opened his eyes: it must be morning. In the half-light of a stone cottage, he watched his mother and sister poking the smouldering peat fire. He listened to them reciting the kindling prayer, that their fire would burn bright and warm.

He said a dressing prayer as he wriggled into his tunic. He whispered a hasty bathing prayer as he splashed his face, and then stood shivering before the peat fire as it sprang to life, spreading its musty scent of both earth and sea.

He set out with his father for a day's work on the hills, and they said the journey blessing and prayed for the protection of their home.

From the day's dawning to its ending, they spoke the herding blessings for their cattle, uttered prayers for the seeds, and gave thanksgivings for family and shelter and food.

At dusk, the boy stretched out his arm and recited an encircling prayer to the great and powerful God of heaven and earth. He called on God as Three-in-One: a Trinity of God the Father, God the Son and God the Holy Spirit, who is greater than all the forces of darkness and evil.

Ancient Celtic Christians believed deeply that God was present in the smallest activities of their lives, and in all Creation, and so they talked with God throughout the day about everything that they did.

Here are some of their prayers, and new ones inspired by them. Use them, as Celtic children once did, secure in the knowledge that God surrounds you with infinite love and care.

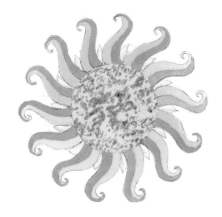

Two Prayers

A low prayer, a high prayer, I send through space.
Arrange them Thyself, O thou King of Grace.

From *The Poem-Book of the Gael*

PRAYERS FOR CREATION

The Lord of Creation

Let us adore the Lord, maker of wondrous works,
great bright Heaven with its angels,
the white-waved sea on earth.

Ninth century Irish

A Prayer of Thanksgiving

I thank the God of Heaven
For rains that soak the Earth.

I thank the Creator of Earth
For food to nourish the World.

I thank the Saviour of the World
For fathers and mothers and children.

I thank the Friend of Children
For all the wonders of Life.

I thank the Spirit of Life
For His abiding Love;
For His abiding Love.

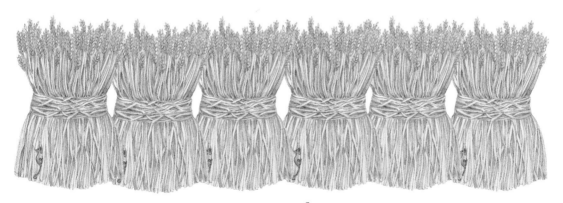

God of All

Our God is the God of all,
The God of heaven and earth,
Of the sea and of the rivers;
The God of the sun and of the moon
And of all the stars;
The God of the lofty mountains
And of the lowly valleys.
He has his dwelling around heaven and earth,
And sea, and all that in them is.

St Patrick

A Prayer for Song Birds

The God of gods protect you
In wind, and hail, and storm;
In summer, keep you cool;
In winter, keep you warm.

The God of gods supply you
With water and with seed,
With perch and branch and house,
And safety as you feed.

The God of gods be watching,
Lest one of you should fall;
Attending every move;
And hearing every call.

The God of gods uplift you,
And speed you in your flight;
Direct you to a sheltered roost,
And keep you snug at night.

The God of gods inspire you,
And fill your heart with song;
Trill greetings in the morning,
And praises all day long.

PRAYERS FOR THE HOME

Blessing of House

God bless the house,
From site to stay,
From beam to wall,
From end to end,
From ridge to basement,
From balk to roof-tree,
From found to summit,
    Found and summit.

From *Carmina Gadelica*

Thanksgiving After Food

Great Giver of the open hand,
We stand to thank Thee for our meat,
A hundred praises, Christ, 'tis meet,
For all we drink, for all we eat.

From *The Poem-Book of the Gael*

PRAYERS FOR LIFE'S JOURNEY

The Pilgrims' Aiding

God be with thee in every pass,
Jesus be with thee on every hill,
Spirit be with thee on every stream,
  Headland and ridge and lawn;

Each sea and land, each moor and meadow,
Each lying down, each rising up,
In the trough of the waves, on the crest of the billows,
  Each step of the journey thou goest.

From *Carmina Gadelica*

A Walking Prayer

Father above me;

Son beside me;

Spirit within me;

The Three all around me.

For Help and Protection

Oh Christ, you calm the storm at sea;
In tempest sore, be calming me.

Oh Christ, you walk upon the wave;
When sinking fast, my footing save.

Oh Christ, the stricken child you raise;
My spirit lift in joy and praise.

Oh Christ, you heal the man born blind;
Make bright the darkness in my mind.

Oh Christ, you feed the crowd with bread;
With words of truth let me be fed.

Oh Christ, you make the water wine;
Take humble gifts and make them fine.

Oh Christ, the Resurrection Morn,
With your new life, my life adorn.

For Comfort

Empty and bereft I be;
I cry to Thee;
Mother me.

Angry and afraid I be;
I long for Thee;
Father me.

Slighted and alone I be;
I reach for Thee;
Stay by me.

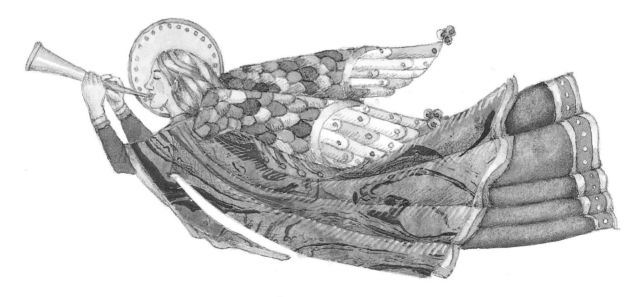

Thwarted and cast down I be;
I turn to Thee;
Hearten me.

Abandoned and forlorn I be;
I run to Thee;
Rescue me.

Grieving and in pain I be;
You come to me,
Explain to me;

You feel for me;
You weep for me;
Redeeming me;
Releasing me.

Peace

Peace between neighbours,
Peace between kindred,
Peace between lovers,
   In the love of the King of life.

Peace between person and person,
Peace between wife and husband,
Peace between woman and children,
   The peace of Christ above all peace.

From *Carmina Gadelica*

Jesus the Encompasser

My Christ! my Christ! my shield, my encircler,
Each day, each night, each light, each dark;
   My Christ! my Christ! my shield, my encircler,
   Each day, each night, each light, each dark.

Be near me, uphold me, my treasure, my triumph,
In my lying, in my standing, in my watching, in my sleeping.

From *Carmina Gadelica* (excerpt from a longer piece)

A Prayer for Journeys

Hear;

Hold;

Love;

Enfold;

God of all hearing;

God of all holding;

God of all loving;

God all enfolding;

Above the winds, hear me;

Upon the sea, hold me;

On lonely isle, love me;

In dark night, enfold me.

PRAYERS OF BLESSING

A Mother's Bed Blessing

Christ's Arm enfold you through the night;
To hold you safe, hold you tight.

Christ's Shield before your covers lay;
To keep the evil powers at bay.

Christ's Hand upon your sleeping head;
To gently comfort you in bed.

Christ's Watch within your dreams tonight;
To soothe your mind, to quell your fright.

Christ's Peace be flooding all your room;
To light the dark, to chase the gloom.

Christ's Love to fill your tender heart;
To hold you fast while we're apart.

I Lie Down
This Night

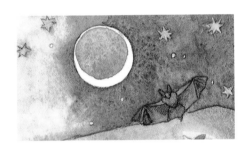

I lie down this night with God,
    And God will lie down with me;
I lie down this night with Christ,
    And Christ will lie down with me;
I lie down this night with Spirit,
    And the Spirit will lie down with me;
God and Christ and the Spirit
    Be lying down with me.

From *Carmina Gadelica*

At Close of Day

Sun rests low beneath the sky;
I beneath my blankets lie;
Father, Son and Spirit, Three,
Be cradling and soothing me.

Lark shouts praises of delight,
Greeting me at early light;
Father, Son and Spirit, Three,
Be welcoming and waking me.

Lily wears her bright array;
I dress with haste to meet the day;
Father, Son and Spirit, Three,
Be covering and assuring me.

Earth laps up the rains that sink;
I take up my food and drink.
Father, Son and Spirit, Three,
Be feeding and refreshing me.

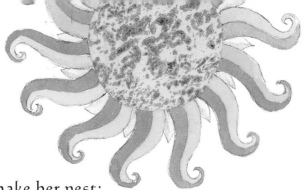

Mouse toils long to make her nest;
I build walls—a place to rest;
Father, Son and Spirit, Three,
Be sheltering and protecting me.

River tumbles on its way;
Dancing on her banks I play;
Father, Son and Spirit, Three,
Be gladdening and cheering me.

Sun again drops to his rest;
Now the quiet when all is blest;
Father, Son and Spirit, Three,
Be blessing and enfolding me.

Father, Son and Spirit, Three,
Encircling sky, encircling sea,
Your circle draw round all of me;
Circle of the Trinity.